Costa del Sol

EVEREST

Text: José Carlos García Rodríguez

Photographs: Miguel Raurich and Oliviero Daidola

Editorial coordination: Francisco Bargiela

Layout: Ana Cristina López

Cover design: Alfredo Anievas

Digital Image Processing: Marcos R. Méndez

Translation: EURO:TEXT (Martin Gell)

© EDITORIAL EVEREST, S.A.
Carretera León-La Coruña, km 5 - LEÓN
ISBN: 84-241-3495-8
Legal deposit: LE. 695-1998
Printed in Spain - Impreso en España

EDITORIAL EVERGRÁFICAS, S.L.
Carretera León-La Coruña, km 5
LEÓN (Spain)

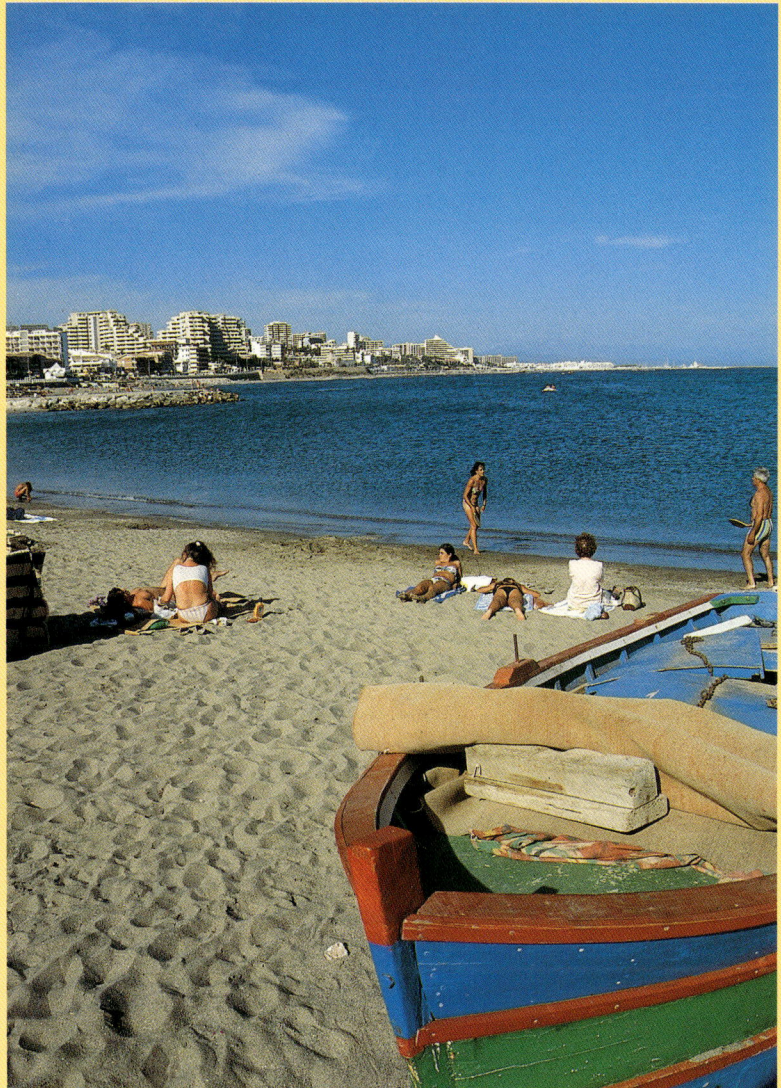

Torremolinos is marked by the contrasts to be found between traditional Andalusia and its tourist resorts, its quiet corners and its mass entertainment, so characteristic of the whole Costa del Sol.

The **Costa del Sol,** facing out into the Mediterranean in the form of a gently curving arch, ranks as the most tourist-oriented coast in Andalusia and boasts the greatest international appeal. Stretching out over 150 kilometres, from the border with the province of Cádiz to **Costa Tropical** in Granada, Costa del Sol is a resort steeped in history, in which the eternal character of Andalusia is linked to the present by the bonds of tradition. It is a place where time, having long come to a standstill, has learnt to live with ever-spiralling urban development, and where havens of peace and quiet still manage to survive amidst what has become a cosmopolitan world devoted to mass entertainment.

This is a land of convergence, one marked by episodes of colonization and conquest, one whose place names evoke a truly fascinating past history, vestiges of which lie tucked away behind magnificent seafront promenades or in the shadow of avant-garde developments and luxury residential complexes, allowing the visitor a glimpse of a past brimming with a myriad of cultures. Sheltered from the inland winds by the Bermeja and Almijara mountains, fanned by the gentle Mediterranean breeze and blessed by seemingly permanent sunny skies, this coastal strip of the province of Málaga is dotted with a succession of villages that have sprawled out beyond their bounds as a result of the relentless tourist boom. Each one of these villages displays its own very distinct identity and together they form the diverse character of the Costa del Sol, a coast designed to cater both for revellers, sports enthusiasts and those simply wishing to unwind. No wonder it has become one of the best-loved holiday destinations amongst foreign tourists.

Preceding two-page spread, night-time view of Casares.

This page, different views of Casares.

The N-340 coastal road, itself a true landmark of the Costa del Sol, leads the traveller into Málaga province from the west through the area known as **Campo de Gibraltar,** which borders on the neighbouring province of Cádiz. Greeting us on this threshold of the Costa del Sol - amidst views of rolling hills and ravines cleft by tiny streams - is the hilltop crowned by **Manilva,** a small farming town renowned for its grapes. In the late 18th century, Manilva was separated from neighbouring **Casares,** the mountainous birthplace of *andalucismo*, the regional identity or spirit of independence championed by Blas Infante, the illustrious son of this beautiful village that exudes an unmistakeably Moorish flavour.

Dotted along this westernmost stretch of the coastline is a succession of beaches that as yet have not been overrun, namely *Playa del Negro, Playa de la Sardina, Playa de las Arenas* and *Playa de Manilva.* Then there is **San Luis de Sabinillas,** a small summer resort whose *Castillo de la Duquesa,* a castle erected in 1767, serves as a reminder of the vulnerability of this coast, which in the past was so often plundered by marauding corsairs.

Outskirts of Manilva.

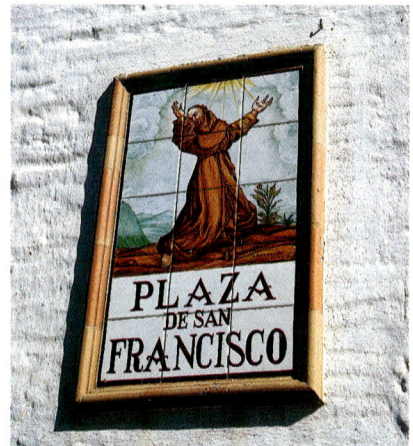

The Old Quarter of Estepona, featuring its immaculate parish church,
balconies decked out with flowers, whitewashed walls and
tile name-plates identifying the local streets and squares.

Eight kilometres from Manilva at the foot of the Bermeja mountains lies **Estepona,** a town that in all likelihood stems from the Iberian settlement of *Salduba* referred to by classical authors and which today is a major tourist resort of the western section of Málaga's coastal region, featuring as it does Roman remains and a marina located between the points **of La Doncella** and **La Plata.**

Despite being bounded by the modern buildings lining the pleasant seafront promenade, the *Old Quarter* of Estepona has managed to preserve its original appearance of a fishing village. Bearing witness to the advent of Chrisitianity in Estepona subsequent to its being conquered by King Henry IV, are the remains of San Luis Castle. In the course of time a succession of towers would be added to reinforce the castle structure, towers that today lend their names to some of the many local beaches and which in times gone by played a vital role on this low-lying sandy coast in warding off the threat of raids perpetrated by Berber pirates from northern Africa.

The contrast between the modern buildings lining Estepona's promenade and the Old Quarter.

Estepona harbour: the town's past as a fishing village is still apparent in today's tourist resort.

Remains of the Palaeochristian Vega del Mar basilica.

Rejoining the ever-busy N-340, we soon come to another major centre for holidaymaking, **San Pedro de Alcántara.** Renowned for the magnificent views provided by its vantage point, San Pedro also features the Palaeochristian Vega del Mar basilica which, dating from the 3rd century, once served as a Visigothic necropolis and today symbolizes the area's historical significance. Administratively speaking, San Pedro belongs to the municipal district of Marbella, lying some 10 km west of the latter. It moreover acts as a gateway leading the traveller into the mountains and along the C-339 road to **Ronda,** a true architectural jewel of the province of Málaga, a town whose historical beauty beckons us along 53 kilometres of winding road flanked by steep, rugged slopes.

San Pedro de Alcántara.

Benadalid, in the Ronda mountains.

Ronda, seen from a distance.

The walls encircling Ronda.

Festive atmosphere in the streets of Ronda.

Marbella is surrounded by luxury residential developments, first-class hotels and sports clubs.

Lit-up scene of Avenida del Mar and its gardens.

The road leading from San Pedro de Alcántara to **Marbella** is a never-ending succession of luxury residential developments, first-class hotels and golf courses. Regarded today as institutions in their own right, **Nueva Andalucía, Los Monteros, Puente Romano, Marbella Club** and **Artola** are the names that first made this part of the coast, nicknamed the *Golden Mile*, internationally famous as an exclusive, quality holiday resort. Featuring as it does a dozen or so golf courses - Río Real, Aloha, Los Naranjos, Las Brisas, La Quinta, Guadalmina Norte y Sur, Dama de Noche, Marbella Golf, Santa María -, the municipal district of Marbella has earnt the distinction of being one of the major destinations in the world for golfing enthusiasts, who can play all year round along this, the *Costa del Golf*. Water sports are catered for in Marbella by no less than three marinas, among them **Puerto Banús,** in the Nueva Andalucía area. Undoubtedly the most famous of all Mediterranean marinas, Puerto Banús boasts a shopping district replete with the most prestigious names from the world of haute couture and fashion design and a number of select restaurants that offer internationally renowned cuisines. Magnificent motor yachts and sailing boats can also be admired at the other two marinas, namely **Club Marítimo de Marbella,** right at the heart of the Promenade, and **Cabopino,** 12 km away on the road to Málaga.

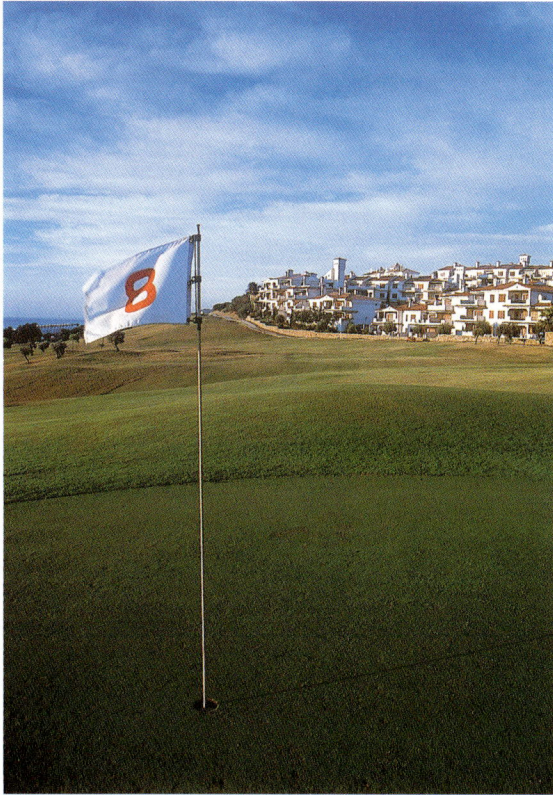

Marbella is also known as "Costa del Golf".

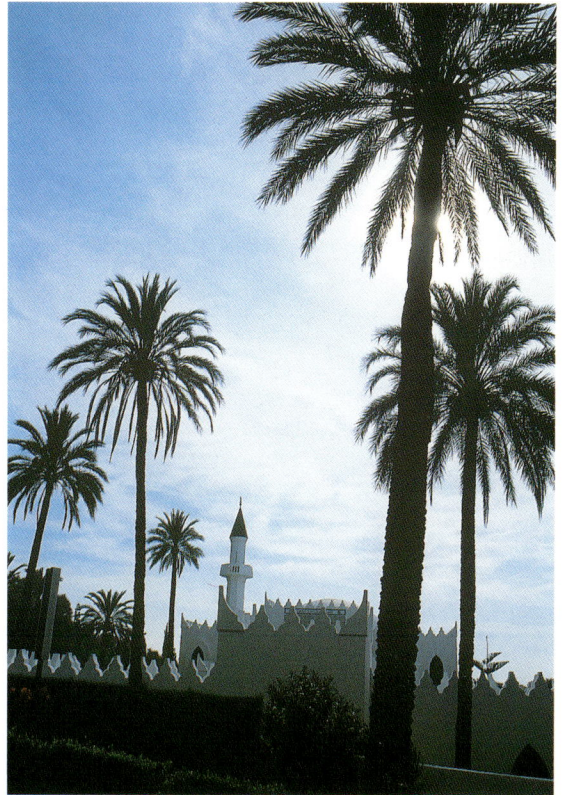

The mosque, another feature of cosmpolitan Marbella.
Puerto Banús.

Marbella Beach.

Marbella's Club Marítimo marina. ➤

Plaza de los Naranjos, flanked by the Town Hall, in Marbella.

Fortunately, alongside this dazzlingly exclusive face of Marbella - famous for its glittering parties, its "beautiful people" who forever grace the national gossip magazines, and its palatial multi-milionaires' residences -, the traditional character of the town has managed to survive, its purity contrasting sharply with such artificiality. Of the original town centre - which was laid out in the style characteristic of villages enjoying a Moorish tradition, with narrow streets lined with two or three-storey whitewashed houses - an attractive group of buildings still remains, clustered around the secluded, landscaped *Plaza de los Naranjos* (Orange-tree Square). Flanking the square are two 16th-century edifices: the town hall or *Casa del Corregidor*, with its beautiful central balcony whose windows feature a double stone framing, and the Hermitage of El Santo Cristo, itself boasting a graceful tower crowned by an octagonal spire. Nearby lies what is the most interesting piece of monumental architecture in Marbella, the parish church of *Nuestra Señora de la Encarnación*, which, dating from 1505, flaunts a beautiful Rococo-style portal crafted from a reddish-hued stone. Remains of what was originally the Roman settlement of Barbesula and subsequently the Arab town of Barbela are to be found at the mouth of the River Verde and also in the shape of two battlemented towers and the Mozarabic castle walls that surround part of Marbella's old quarter. As far as the local museums are concerned, one should not miss the *Museo del Grabado Español* (Spanish Engraving Museum) housed in the *Hospital Bazán*, itself a building of great historical importance, and the *Museo de Bonsais* (Bonsai Museum), which was opened recently in a modern building at the Arroyo de Represa Park. Once again, in Marbella, the visitor senses the call of the nearby mountains. By taking the road to Coín, which leads us through a landscape of steeply rising terrain, the source of streams whose waters tumble merrily down to the sea, we come to **Ojén,** a village which, famous for its eau-de-vie, peeks out from amidst pinewoods and eucalyptus groves on a craggy slope in the foothills of the Blanca and Alpujata mountains. Awaiting us beyond Ojén is **Monda,** a picturesque village that endured great suffering during the Moorish revolts and which may well have once been *Munda*, the site of the decisive battle fought between the troops of Caesar and Pompey. **Coín,** 29 kilometres from Marbella, is a town that, alongside its time-honoured pottery tradition, boasts a thriving agriculture founded on Arab irrigation techniques. Originally established by the Moslems, the town was once defended by a mighty fortress and today features a varied monumental heritage. Outstanding examples of the latter are the two 16th-century local parish churches, *San Andrés*, also known as *La Caridad* (having once belonged to the La Caridad hospital), and *San Juan Bautista*, along with the Hermitage of La Virgen de la Fuensanta, situated at **Cruz de Piedra** and adorned by beautiful stuccowork.

Three of Marbella's characteristic corners.

Below, Marbella Castle.

Opposite, Church of Nuestra Señora de la Encarnación (Marbella).

Hermitage of San Sebastián.
An institution amongst tourists: the "burro taxi".

As we make our way back to the coast along the road leading to Fuengirola, we pass through **Alhaurín el Grande,** a town that affords marvellous views from its vantage point out over the green meadowland lining the banks of the River Guadalhorce. As part of the Holy Week celebrations, the two rival local confraternities, one sporting green attire, the other violet, will be seen parading the streets. Our next stop after Alhaurín is **Mijas,** acclaimed in promotional brochures as being the true *essence of Andalusia.* A residential tourist resort whose fame has spread halfway round the world, Mijas is the centre of a district that, as one can appreciate from the 1,150 m-high vantage point, sweeps down from the mountains bearing its name to the beaches of *Cala Moral, Butibamba, Calahonda* and *El Chaparral,* which themselves stretch out over a distance of 12 km. Mijas was awarded its town charter by Charles I in reward for the loyalty shown during the *Comunero* uprisings. Despite being continually invaded by an avalanche of tourists, the town constitutes a fine illustration of how urban development need not be detrimental to the environment. Indeed, exemplary urbanistic legislation has been adhered to, right down to the very design of the modern residential developments that have sprung up all over the district, thereby preserving the picturesque character of one of the most attractive towns of the Costa del Sol. Consequently, visitors to the town are afforded so much more than the rather touristy *burro taxi* and the *Carromato de Max* museum of miniature curiosities, two of the town's most popular and best-known attractions.

The vernacular architecture of Mijas, best preserved in the winding streets of the upper part of town, displays a marked Arab influence, the fruit of the long Moslem occupation of the town, which began upon its conquest in 714 by 'Abd al-Aziz, son of Islamic ruler Musa b Nusayr. Urbanisitically speaking, this a town of notable balance and serenity, featuring a number of pleasant, welcoming squares such as *Plaza de la Constitución, Plaza de la Libertad* and *Plaza de los Siete Caños.* Indeed, Mijas enjoys great popularity amongst the tourists staying at other resorts along the coast, many of whom, captivated by the singular atmosphere of a town that belongs to both the mountains and the sea, choose to live here on a permanent basis, amidst the friendly environment of the traditionally very hospitable local population.

Mijas is renowned for its urban development, which has shown great respect for both the environment and tradition. Above, in the background, the Parish Church of La Inmaculada Concepción.

Two-page spread overleaf, Fuengirola Beach.

Fuengirola.

Fuengirola.

Although not quite able to match the cosmopolitan air of neighbouring Marbella, the busy town of **Fuengirola,** whose tiny municipal district is almost entirely built-up, nevertheless ranks amongst the major resorts gracing the Costa del Sol. Having originally been called *Suel* by the Phoenicians, it was subsequently renamed *Sohail* by the Arabs, in honour of a star belonging to the Argos constellation which, as legend will have it, could only be seen from the castle erected by 'Abd al-Rahman III, an edifice that today stands as a reminder of Fuengirola's past history.

From the early 'seventies onwards, Fuengirola district was to take full advantage of the tourist boom that hit the coastal region of Málaga and consequently underwent a period of immense growth, apparent today in its vast cluster of apartment blocks, hotels and residential developments. The long promenade and the central beaches of Carvajal, Egido, Los Boliches, Las Gaviotas, Santa Amalia and El Castillo represent the area's main attractions and are much frequented by local people in search of relaxation. Fuengirola boasts another, more recent promenade, Los Boliches, the highlight of which is a successfully reconstructed Roman temple whose façade was discovered quite by chance on a building site.

Lying just two kilometres from Fuengirola, **Santa Fe de los Boliches,** whose appearance is that typical of a small fishing village, still exudes the quintessential flavour of the architecture characteristic of Mediterranean Andalusia.

Fuengirola. Promenade.

Fuengirola Castle.

Benalmádena Marina.

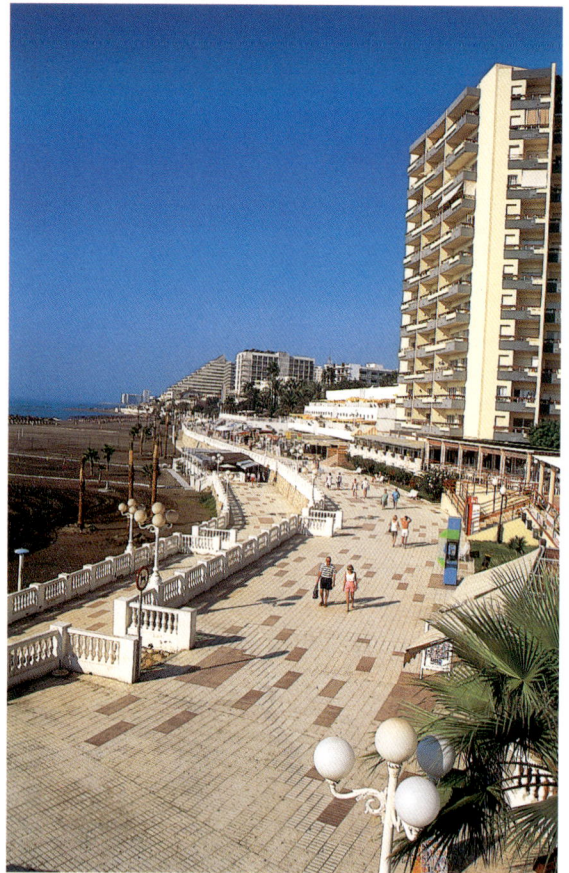

Promenade.

On leaving Fuengirola, as we head for the major city on the Costa del Sol, Málaga, we come across Benalmádena, whose reconstructed, well-kept original village can still be seen crowning a hill 3 kilometres inland from the coast.

In recent times the focus of attention in **Benalmádena** has shifted from the village to the beaches lining its coast. Having been an important stronghold during the Moslem occupation - the meaning of the town's name in Arabic being *"children of the mine"* -, this is the birthplace of the famous apothecary Ibn al-Bethar, who lived in the late 12th, early 13th centuries and was appointed as doctor to Saladin, sultan of Egypt.

Benalmádena-Costa, which is the name given to the town's seafront district, ranks as one of the liveliest spots of the coastal region of Málaga, featuring as it does a wide variety of leisure facilities, including a casino, a marina, a cultural centre at the Neo-Moorish Bil Bil castle, and even a fairground, *Tívoli*, to be found at Arroyo de la Miel, halfway between the coast and Benalmádena village. Standing at the entrance to the village is the interesting local Archaeological Museum, which displays a number of Neolithic items and a fine collection of ceramics and other articles belonging to the pre-Columbian cultures of several South American countries.

As is the case with most towns along the Costa del Sol, the beaches at Benalmádena - Carvajal, La Morera, Torremuelle, Arroyo Hondo, Viborillas, Torrequebrada, Torre Vigía and Torre Bermeja - take their names from the watchtowers erected along the coast as from the 16th century.

Benalmádena Beach.

Benalmádena, the popular "little girl" statue.

La Carihuela Beach in Torremolinos.
Preceding two-page spread, hill-top view of Benalmádena.

El Bajondillo Beach (Torremolinos).

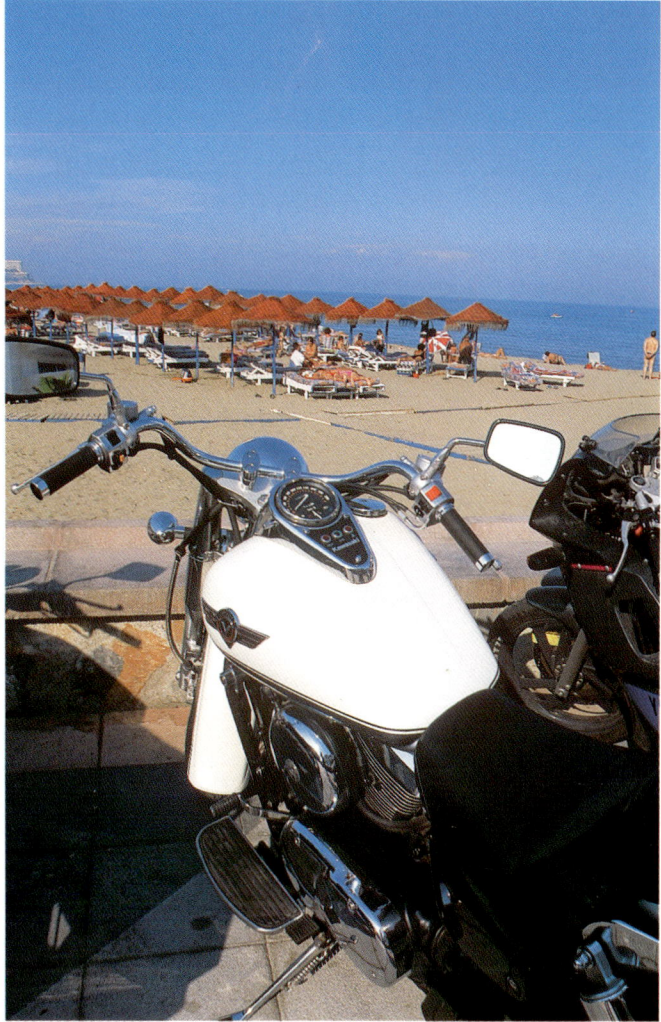

La Carihuela Beach.

Torremolinos, 12 km east of Benalmádena, is essentially a haven for beachlovers, its coastline stretching right from Saltillos to El Retiro before concluding at the mouth of the River Guadalhorce. Its beaches - La Carihuela, El Bajondillo, Montemar and El Lido - enjoy a magnificent reputation amongst holidaymakers, both Spanish and foreign, who flock here in search of sun and fun in a setting brimming with local colour. Lying at the foot of the *Sierra de Mijas*, at a point where the coastline juts out into the sea, Torremolinos can boast but a very short history. It is just over a hundred years old and until very recently came under the administration of Málaga. Its name derives from *Torre Pimentel*, a tower erected to keep watch over this part of the coast, and the mills (*Sp., molinos*) that dotted the surrounding area. Right from the beginning of the tourist boom that in the name of economic progress irreversibly changed the face of the Mediterranean coast of Andalusia, Torremolinos has enjoyed a mythical status on the Costa del Sol. Owing to the marvellous local climate and the proximity of both the city of Málaga and its international airport, what was formerly a fishing village located in the El Bajondillo and La Carihuela districts would in time undergo a development that has surpassed even the wildest of dreams. Today, Torremolinos is a sprawling succession of hotels, apartment buildings and residential complexes such as Las Lomas, Miramar, La Nogalera, Playamar, Eurosol and Montemar, the latter having brought about the immense expansion of this most cosmopolitan of resorts, one whose most popular street, the bustling *Calle de San Miguel*, is held by many, owing to its international flavour, to constitute a modern-day Tower of Babel.

Torremolinos, regarded as the antithesis of Marbella on account of the more down-market holidays it offers, boasts a wide range of leisure facilities ranging from waterparks to golf courses and, thanks to its Congress and Exhibition Centre, it also acts as a venue for business conventions. The exquisite local cuisine, featuring traditional dishes and the popular *fritos marineros* or fried seafood, can be sampled at restaurants in La Carihuela.

Torremolinos Congress Centre.

Shining waters at Torremolinos.

Torremolinos is famous for its night-life. Above, La Carihuela Beach; opposite, El Bajondillo Beach.

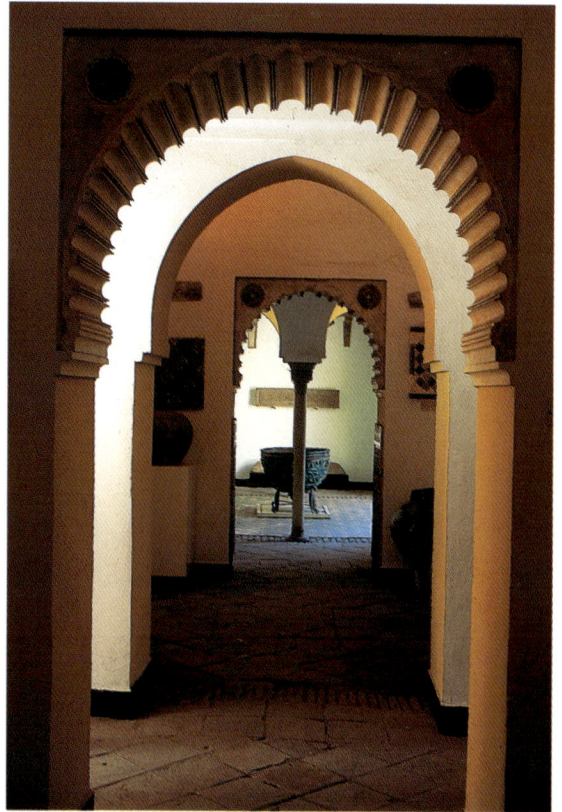

Málaga is a city steeped in history. Having been a confederate town in Roman times, it subsequently became a major Moslem settlement. The photograph on the left shows the former Roman theatre, whilst the one on the right is a view of the Arab fortress or Alcazaba.

Next, our journey brings us to **Málaga,** the only true city on the Costa del Sol, commanded by the Gibralfaro hill - whence its former name of *Malaka*, which simply means "hill covered in pastures" - and cleft into two by the River Guadalmedina - which, more a stream than a river, often swells up lest anyone should forget its presence. Featuring a population of around 600,000, Málaga is steeped in history. In Roman times it was a confederate town governed by a special code of laws - the so-called *lex flavia malacitana*. Subsequently it was to become a major Moslem settlement, vestiges of which still survive in the shape of the Alcazaba and the Gibralfaro fortifications.

Paseo del Parque, an avenue graced by a 19th-century botanical garden, and its continuation, *Alameda Principal,* a French-style walkway dating from the reign of Charles III, constitute the true backbone of Málaga's urban layout. Flanked by buildings such as the City Hall and the former Customs' House - today home to the representation of the Spanish government -, this area is also the hub of all administrative activity in the city. Leading off from here, away from the Mediterranean and the port that brought intense activity to the city, a number of streets such as Marqués de Larios, Molina Larios, Puerta del Mar and Nueva eventually converge on *Plaza de la Constitución.* This square marks the heart of the traditional commercial district of Málaga, an area that borders on the old medieval quarter, itself brimming with monumental buildings of a religious and artistic nature, such as the churches of *San Juan, Los Mártires, San Felipe Neri, Santísimo Cristo de la Salud, San Agustín* and *Santiago,* as well as Las Atarazanas (the Shipyards), San Julián Hospital and the magnificent Cathedral, commonly referred to by the locals as *"manquita"* (one-armed), owing to the fact that one of its towers remains unfinished.

Plaza de la Merced, lying adjacent to the site of what was the *Puerta de Granada* gateway in the walls that once encircled Málaga, is one of the town's most charming squares. Here, the visitor is reminded of the episode in which General José María Torrijos and his liberal followers were shot dead by absolutist forces on the sands of Playa de San Andrés in 1831. Their remains lie buried beneath the square, solemnly guarded by a commemorative obelisk. Likewise giving onto *Plaza de la Merced* is the Picasso Birthplace Foundation, soon to feature a museum, which gives us an insight into the private life and the work of the world-renowned local painter, who first developed his artistic genius right here in Málaga.

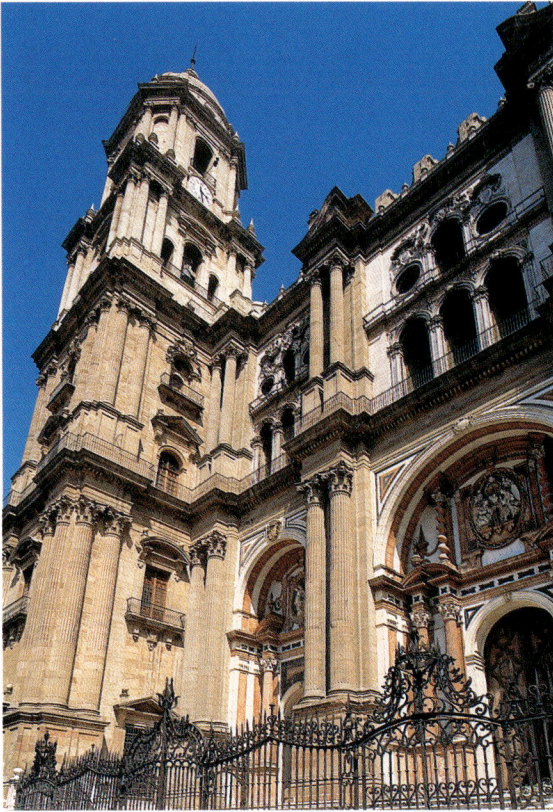

Málaga Cathedral.

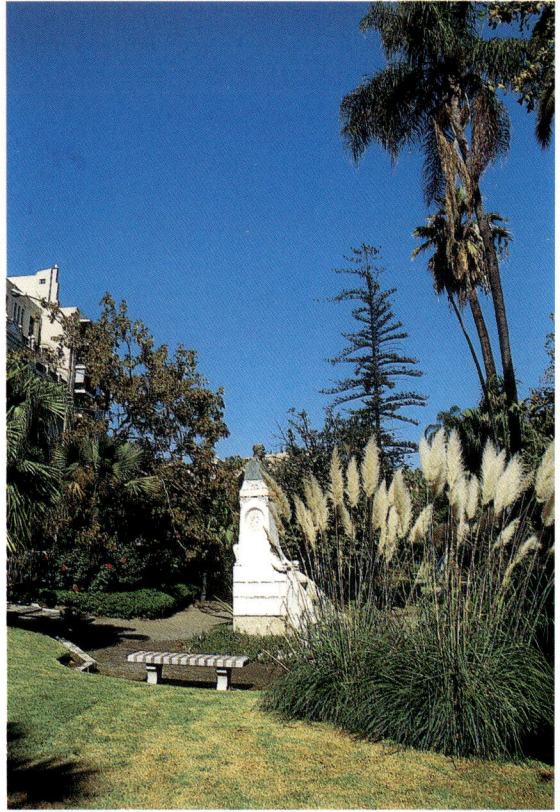

Paseo del Parque.

City Hall.

Picasso's birthplace.

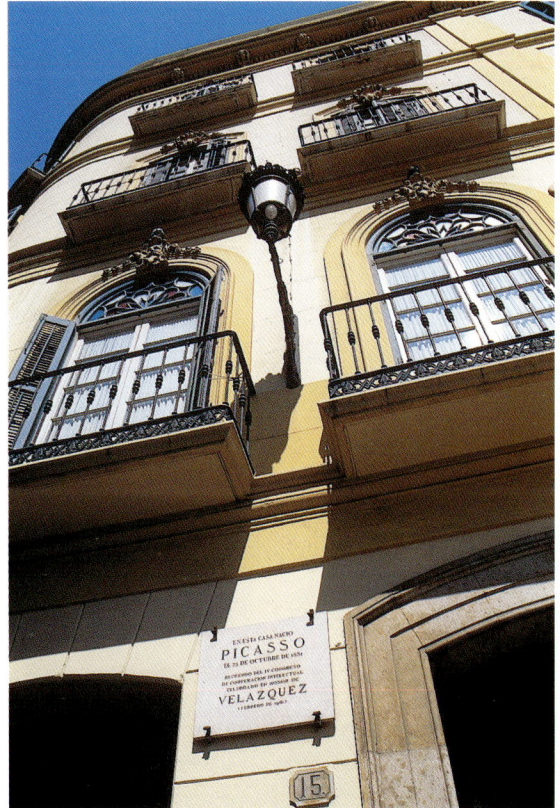

Two-page spread overleaf: La Malagueta district and the view to the east. ➤

The port of Málaga seen at different times of day.

Sunset over the port.

La Malagueta Beach and its promenade.

Alongside the bourgeois face of Málaga that once flourished in the form of the now dilapidated Sevillian, pseudo-French and modernist-style mansions lining *Paseo de Reding*, an avenue that opened up a whole new area of the town beyond *La Malagueta*, the visitor will also enjoy the character of districts such as *El Palo*, dotted with fishermen's dwellings, and *El Perchel*, quoted by Cervantes as being the quintessence of Andalusia, neighbourhoods which retain, in all its purity, the delightful atmosphere characteristic of Málaga. This ambience is often tinged with grandeur, as is seen on the occasion of major religious events, the most outstanding of which are the Holy Week processions featuring exuberantly decorated floats, and on that of Málaga's pagan rituals, such as the spectacular festival of Flamenco song and dance called *Los Verdiales* and the local August Fair. No less grandiose is the local cuisine, whose pièce de résistance is undoubtedly the renowned fried seafood or *fritura malagueña*.

Different scenes illustrating Málaga's festivities and traditions, from Holy Week to the Fair.

El Cenachero (monument to basket-carriers).

Rincón de la Victoria.

La Axarquía. Daimalis.

Beyond Málaga, the beaches of the Costa del Sol are similarly blessed with shallow, tranquil waters; this stretch of the coast, however, enjoys a greater degree of privacy, and those in search of peace and quiet will find it here in a series of tiny whitewashed villages, against the backdrop of an altogether much more subdued landscape.

As we follow the coastline eastwards - along what is called the *Costa del Sol Oriental* -, the first town we come to is that of **Rincón de la Victoria,** which, some 12 km from Málaga along the N-340, marks the beginning of the historical region of **La Axarquía.** Formerly the Arab town of *Bizmiliana*, Rincón de la Victoria is set against a landscape dominated by the foothills of the Montes de Málaga. Today the town has successfully managed to combine its new role as a summer resort with its time-honoured devotion to the fishing trade.

Examples of cave art and several items belonging to the Palaeolithic have been discovered at *Cueva del Higuerón,* which, situated just outside the town, is also called *Cueva del Tesoro* ("Treasure Cave") on account of the legend according to which five Hammudis, attempting to flee from their pursuing enemy, hid a large amount of gold in the cave.

Vélez-Málaga. In the background, the castle.

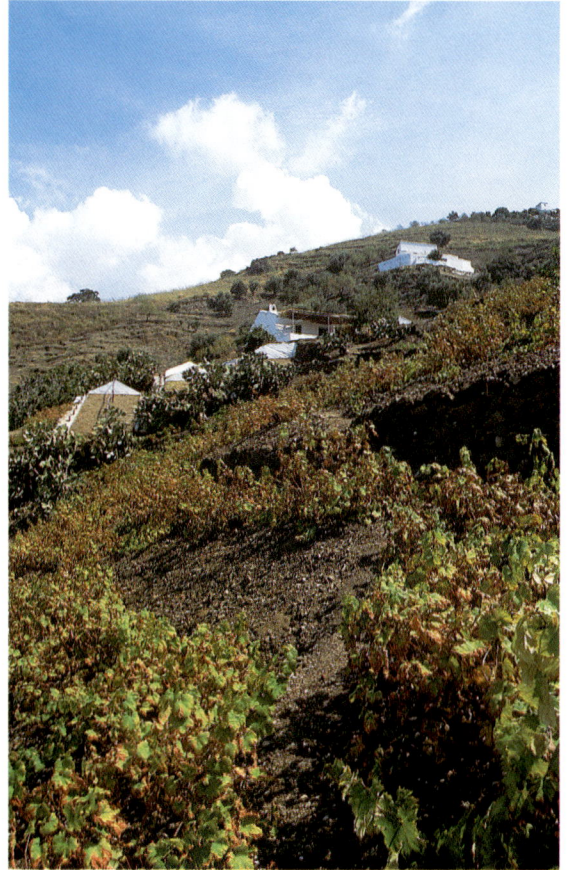

The landscape of La Axarquía.

As we continue our journey along the Costa del Sol, it is well worth taking time out to visit **Vélez-Málaga,** which, having a population of over 50,000, is the capital of the region of La Axarquía. Whilst all evidence would suggest that the town originally evolved from the Greek settlement of *Mainake* and is a direct successor of the Arab town of *Ballix-Malaca* ("Fortress of Málaga"), Vélez-Málaga owes its present-day name to the river that bathes its extensive valley, where vineyards, olive groves and sugar-cane plantations are all seen to thrive.

The evolution of Vélez-Málaga throughout the centuries is reflected in the array of monumental structures that lie scattered around the districts of San Sebastián, El Ensanche and La Villa. Overlooking the town are the remains of its former Castle, of which the keep and parts of the walls stand as a reminder of the vital role played by the fortress in the Moslem defence of the kingdom of Granada. Amongst the buildings erected subsequent to the reconquest of Vélez-Málaga by King Ferdinand the Catholic in 1487 are the churches of Santa María la Mayor and San Juan, the former erected over a mosque, and the San Marcos Hospital. Finally, the one-time mansion, *Palacio de los Marqueses de Veniel*, which today houses a municipal administration offices, is a secular edifice whose balconies and iron grillework are true illustrations of the town's traditional architecture.

During the Spanish War of Succession, the Vélez-Málaga coast was the scene of a naval battle in which a French squadron under the Count of Toulouse defeated an English formation commanded by Admiral Rooke. Along its shore, a line of defensive towers was erected to keep watch over waters that during the 16th and 17th centuries were frequently threatened by Turkish and Berber raids. Amongst the towers still surviving today are *Torre de Chilches, Torre Moya,* the so-called *Castillo del Marqués* and *Torre Manganeta.*

Lying some 4 km from Vélez is the village of Torre del Mar, which is in effect the seaboard continuation of the latter, a tourist haven featuring a succession of beaches stretching from **Chilches** to Punta de Torrox.

Torre del Mar.

Two-page spread overleaf, the port of Caleta de Vélez.

Torrox Beach.

Fishermen at Nerja.

Algarrobo, 11 km east of Vélez-Málaga, is another inland town that boasts a satellite coastal resort. Clearly dating back to Moslem times, it features a perfect urban layout, one that is characteristic of the villages of La Axarquía.

Torrox, which likewise so jealously guards the vestiges of its past under Moslem occupation, takes pride in having been the place where 'Abd al-Rahman sought refuge after landing at Almuñecar in 755. Sheltered by the Tejeda and Almijara mountains, the town was established inland, where it enjoyed better protection against raids by pirates that lay in wait in Algiers. Today, Torrox is an important centre for the production of raisins and subtropical foods such as mangos, custard apples, bananas and sugar cane, all of which thrive thanks to the water supplied by the River Torrox, the largest of those flowing through the area.

Just 5 km from Torrox, nestling in the last foothills of the Almijara and Tejeda mountains, the town of **Nerja** marks the eastern boundary of the region of La Axarquía and with it the end of the Costa del Sol. Graced with a coastline of sheer cliffs and an abundance of points, inlets and coves, Nerja ranks as the major tourist resort on the eastern stretch of the Costa del Sol. Nevertheless, from an architectural point of view, Nerja has little in common with the rest of the holiday spots along the Málaga coast. On the contrary, as far as urban development is concerned, it has displayed a continuing respect for what it regards as its own traditional features.

A highlight of Nerja is its Balcón de Europa, a splendid lookout point in the shape of a rotunda, which affords picture-postcard views out over the sea. Rowing, angling and dragnet fishing are typical activities in Nerja, a common sight being that of the local fishing-boats drawing in their nets (*seines*) to the Burriana and Calahorra beaches. Nerja is also renowned for its many unspoilt mountainous nature spots, whose colours are simply beyond compare and which exude a fragrance of rosemary, honeysuckle and jasmine. The peaceful streets of Nerja lead us down to the shore and the highly nostalgic seafront areas of La Caletilla, El Salón, El Boquete de Calahonda and El Chorrillo, where some fishermen's dwellings still stand today. On venturing inland, we come across farming lands blessed with clement weather and an abundance of water, a landscape dominated by the green of the sugar-cane plantations that in the past supplied a number of local sugar refineries which have now all but disappeared.

Nerja. ➤

Buildings of outstanding historical interest are few and far between in Nerja, whose main attraction would seem to lie in the very beauty of its simple, balanced appearance. The structure that best represents the traditional character of the town is its whitewashed parish church, *El Salvador*, which, completed in the 18th century, features an adjoining tower crowned by an octagonal spire. Likewise Baroque in style, the Hermitage of La Virgen de las Angustias has a number of interesting paintings adorning its vaults and squinches.

It is a must for any visitor to stroll through the streets surrounding *El Salvador*, the true nucleus of 18th-century Nerja. This district is the heart of what in former times was a thriving agricultural town, one that was devoted to its fertile lowlands and nearby leafy woods. Every inch of these streets is reminiscent of the great prosperity that was enjoyed by Nerja until the arrival of ridiculously cheap sugar from the Caribbean brought to an end the riches produced by the local refineries.

Nerja is doubtless more universally known for its famous cave, which is to be found in limestone rock projecting out of the mountain chain to which the *Sierra de Almijara belongs.* Discovered by chance in the vicinity of some terraces that in 1957 were recovered from the peasants' district of *Maro* for the planting of sugar-cane, the renowned *Cueva de Nerja* is one of the most impressive natural attractions of the Costa del Sol. As well as being an important archaeological site, having been inhabited as early as the Palaeolithic, the cave is also an extraordinary auditorium, one in which a number of festivals, held against the marvellous backdrop of stalactites and stalagmites, have brought a whole new dimension to the worlds of music and dance.

Boat on the beach at Nerja. ➤

Calahonda Beach and the Balcón de Europa lookout point.

Local handicrafts displayed on the whitewashed walls in the narrow streets of Frigiliana.

Frigiliana, a town untouched by the tourist and building boom that has swept across the Costa del Sol, lies 5 km inland from Nerja, with which it enjoys certain historical links. Irrigated by the rapid-flowing waters of the River Higuerón and standing over 400 m above sea level in the *Sierra de Enmedio* mountains, Frigiliana boasts a Moorish-Mudéjar-style old quarter which, regarded as the best preserved in all Andalusia, is a fine illustration of what is perhaps the most pleasant and peaceful aspect of the coastal region of Málaga. Having inherited the legacy of ancient settlements, Frigiliana was an important focus of Arab revolt in the days subsequent to the conquest of the area by King Ferdinand the Catholic, a time when the Moslem population was subjected to great pressure. The Moorish rebels flocked together in this town, but were defeated in the Battle of the Rock of Frigiliana, whereupon they were expelled from Spain in 1569.

Set amidst the whitewashed dwellings of Frigiliana's narrow, twisting, steeply rising streets that face out to the carefully tended farmland terraces, a number of noteworthy buildings remain, such as the former royal silo (called *Antiguo Pósito*), the Baroque parish church of San Antonio and the 16th-century residence of the Manrique de Lara family, who held the title of counts of Frigiliana.

Those who visit Frigiliana inevitably come to the conclusion that the Costa del Sol far surpasses any expectations one might have harboured in light of the image projected by its tourist brochures and the package holidays provided for the mass market. As we stand atop the silent mountains, looking out over the coastline that disappears at *Cerro Gordo*, the hill marking the provincial border with Granada, we perceive the true grandeur of these timeless lands of Andalusia that in the course of history were to receive a constant influx of new peoples, cultures and ways of life. Today, as always, Andalusia welcomes its visitors with open arms, greeting them with a hospitality acquired in the course of thousands of years.